AIRCRAFT

Hurricane Hunters

Timothy R. Gaffney

Enslow Publishers, Inc.

40 Industrial Road   PO Box 38
Box 398   Aldershot
Berkeley Heights, NJ 07922   Hants GU12 6BP
USA   UK

http://www.enslow.com

Library of Congress Cataloging-in-Publication Data

Gaffney, Timothy R.
    Hurricane hunters / Timothy R. Gaffney.
        p. cm. — (Aircraft)
    Includes bibliographical references and index.
    ISBN 0-7660-1569-6
      1. Aeronautics in meteorology—Juvenile literature. 2. Hurricanes—Research—Juvenile literature. [1. Hurricanes. 2. Meteorology. 3. Airplanes.]
    I. Title. II. Series.
    QC879.35 .G34   2001
    551.55'2'072073—dc21

                                    00-011259

Printed in the United States of America

10 9 8 7 6 5 4 3 2

To Our Readers: We have done our best to make sure all Internet addresses in this book were active and appropriate when we went to press. However, the author and the publisher have no control over and assume no liability for the material available on those Internet sites or on other Web sites they may link to. Any comments or suggestions can be sent by e-mail to comments@enslow.com or to the address on the back cover.

Photo Credits: © Corel Corporation, pp. 3, 12, 18, 22, 33; Timothy R. Gaffney, p. 27; National Aeronautics and Space Administration (NASA), pp. 7, 34, 35, 37, 39, 41; National Oceanic and Atmospheric Administration (NOAA), pp. 8, 23, 24, 25, 28, 29, 30, 31; MSgt. Michele Rivera, USAFR 403rd Wing, pp. 4–5, 10, 14, 17, 19, 20; United States Air Force, pp. 15, 16.

Cover Photo: NASA (background); Lockheed Martin Corporation (inset).

Contents

1-9-03 Enslow Pub Inc. $18.95

CHAPTER 1

Into the Eye

WC-130 Hercules

The four propellers of a large gray U.S. Air Force airplane spin to life. The airplane takes off with six people aboard. It begins a long flight out to sea, straight toward a furious hurricane.

The sky is clear where they are flying, but white thunderstorm clouds tower in the distance. The airplane lumbers on until it plunges into a spiral arm of thunderstorms. It is dark inside the clouds. The ride gets bumpy. Raindrops make a sizzling sound as they strike the airplane's metal hull at hundreds of miles an hour. The most violent part of the storm churns ahead, but the airplane does not turn back.

It is not an accident. This airplane is a WC-130 Hercules. It belongs to the Air Force Reserve's 53rd Weather Reconnaissance Squadron, the Hurricane Hunters. The squadron is based at Keesler Air Force Base near Biloxi, Mississippi. Flying through hurricanes is its mission.

Hurricane hunting is a life-or-death mission—not just for the crews, but also for people on land and at sea. Hurricanes can threaten America's coastlines anywhere from Texas to Maine. In an average three-year period, about five hurricanes strike the U.S. coastline. They kill from fifty to one hundred people, according to the U.S. National Oceanic and Atmospheric Administration (NOAA).[1]

In 1992, Hurricane Andrew killed twenty-three people. It caused more than 26 billion dollars' worth of damage in Florida and Louisiana. Its fierce winds destroyed more than 25,000 homes and damaged many more. It left more than a quarter of a million people temporarily homeless.[2]

≡ Eyes on the Storm

Hurricanes form at sea, where it is not easy to keep an eye on them. Satellites help, but Hurricane Hunters gather the most precise data. They do it by flying right through a storm with special devices that measure the storm's strength, size, and movement.

The Hurricane Hunters radio the data directly to NOAA's National Hurricane Center in Miami, Florida. The data helps weather forecasters know how strong the storm is, which way it is headed, and how fast it is moving.

The information is crucial for timely warnings to evacuate or take cover. As destructive as Hurricane Andrew was, the Hurricane Hunters helped prevent it

The U.S. Air Force Reserve's 53rd Weather Reconnaissance Squadron flies the WC-130 Hercules airplane through hurricanes.

from catching people by surprise and causing even greater loss of life.[3]

The Air Force Reserve's Hurricane Hunters are not the only ones who use airplanes to probe hurricanes. There can be several airplanes flying in, around, or over a hurricane at the same time.

NOAA has a fleet of WP-3D Orion airplanes that also fly through hurricanes. They gather more detailed data about the nature of hurricanes than the Hurricane Hunters do. NOAA also flies a small jet around and over hurricanes. It gathers data to help scientists learn how a hurricane is affected by the weather conditions

Hurricanes, such as Hurricane Mitch shown here, threaten the American coast every year. Almost the entire storm can be seen here, with the eye in the center.

around it. NASA, the National Aeronautics and Space Administration, sometimes sends its ER-2 environmental research jet high over a hurricane to study it from the edge of space. You will read about all these planes in Chapters 4 and 5.

≡ A Comforting Sight

The Air Force's weather squadron flies the most frequent hurricane missions. When a tropical storm is within a day or two of reaching the Caribbean islands, Hurricane Hunter airplanes fly in the storm around the clock. As soon as one Hercules leaves, another takes its place.

"It's rather a comforting sight to see the blinking lights of another Hurricane Hunter plane as we pass each other in the middle of the night, as one plane is going out to take the other's place," says Air Force Reserve Major Valerie Hendry.

Hendry knows what it is like inside a hurricane. She has been a Hurricane Hunter since 1985. Her job as the crew's weather officer is to measure conditions inside hurricanes.

"While other airplanes always try to avoid thunderstorms, we sometimes have to fly right through them on our way into the eye. That's where our job really gets interesting," Hendry says. "The airplane engines are very loud, but after a while you don't really notice it . . . until we hit turbulence. Then the engine noise changes as the plane bucks and surges. It gets quite dark inside the thick clouds, and the rain hisses as it stings the

Major Valerie Hendry, a weather officer, has been flying into hurricanes since 1985. She is one of several female crew members who fly with the Hurricane Hunters.

airplane. The rain is so heavy, it's almost as if someone is shooting a firehose at the windows."

The storm gets worse until the airplane reaches the very center. There it finds a calm, clear patch called the eye. "The darkness suddenly begins to lift, and then daylight bursts into the plane," Hendry says. "You feel your spirit soar, knowing you've survived one of nature's worst phenomena."[4]

Hurricanes usually develop over the tropical Atlantic Ocean between June 1 and November 30. A hurricane begins as a tropical depression. This is a large, rotating system of clouds and thunderstorms with winds below 38 miles per hour. When its winds are between 38 and 74 miles an hour, it is known as a tropical storm. When winds stay at 74 miles an hour or higher, it becomes a hurricane. (Hurricanes have different names in different parts of the world. In the western Pacific, they are called typhoons. In the Indian Ocean, they are called cyclones.)[5]

Hurricanes are not the only storms in which Hurricane Hunters fly. Between November and mid-April, they fly through winter storms off both coasts for the National Center for Environmental Prediction. They also may fly through Pacific Ocean storms that might threaten the Hawaiian Islands. On those missions, they gather data for the Central Pacific Hurricane Center in Honolulu.[6]

The Hurricane Hunter mission is one of the many ways airplanes help scientists study weather and Earth's atmosphere.

CHAPTER 2

Tough Planes for a Tough Job

*H*urricane hunting started on a dare. In July 1943, several pilots were on their lunch break from a flight school in Bryan, Texas. Their talk turned to an approaching hurricane. They wondered when they would have to evacuate their AT-6 Texan training planes. Some pilots who flew bigger planes did not believe the single-engine, two-seat Texans could handle stormy weather.

Lieutenant Colonel Joe Duckworth disagreed. He was an AT-6 instructor pilot. He thought the little planes could survive a hurricane. The other pilots dared him to prove it. Duckworth took a navigator with him, and they flew right into the hurricane. They fought turbulence and pounding rain until they reached the eye. They flew a few circles inside it and returned home.

Most pilots would have felt lucky to be back on the ground. Duckworth, however, was ready to go again. This time, the base weather officer joined him. Duckworth flew back into the storm while the weather officer took notes.[1]

For the first time, an airplane had been used to gather information from inside a hurricane. The Army created the first weather reconnaissance squadron just a year later. The history of hurricane hunting had started.

≡ The Power of the Storm

Hurricanes can destroy buildings as if they were only dollhouses. How can airplanes survive them?

"If we were on the ground, the winds would flip our plane over and destroy it," Major Valerie Hendry says. An airplane in flight is a different matter. From an airplane's point of view, flying through calm air at 100 miles per hour feels the same as flying into a hurricane-force wind. In a hurricane, the pilots use their controls to keep the airplane steady as the winds change direction and speed.[2]

Those changes can be dramatic. A plane may fly from a powerful updraft into a powerful downdraft. At times, "it feels like the airplane is falling out from under you," says Air Force Reserve Major Travis White, a WC-130 pilot. "It's almost like a roller coaster."[3]

Pilots Major Eric Roberts (left) and Lieutenant Colonel Floyd Plash keep the aircraft straight and level, on course through Hurricane Lenny in November 1999.

For many years, bombers were the favored airplanes for hurricane hunting missions. Bombers were big enough to carry bulky storm-measuring instruments. They also could fly very long distances. The first, in 1945, was the famous Boeing B-17 Flying Fortress. Other bombers used for hurricane hunting included the North American Aviation B-25 Mitchell, the Boeing B-29 (and its close cousin the B-50) Superfortress, and the Boeing B-47 Stratojet. Starting with the B-29, the military began identifying weather-mission airplanes with a *W*. For example, a hurricane hunting B-29 became a WB-29.

The Air Force ended the bomber tradition in 1963 when it gave the Hurricane Hunters their first C-130s. These were cargo planes built to fly troops and cargo into combat zones and take off from rough airstrips. The C-130 had a well-deserved nickname: Hercules.[4]

The Hercules C-130

The husky, stubby-nosed "Herk" would never win an airplane beauty contest, but the Hurricane Hunters respect it. "It's a very rugged airplane and can stay airborne a long time. Most of our flights last ten to twelve hours," Major Hendry says.

The rugged C-130 is used for hurricane hunting. It is also a cargo plane, with room for many supplies.

The C-130 was a good choice for other reasons, too. "The Air Force already had many C-130 airplanes for carrying cargo, and it had the supply system and people experienced in flying and fixing them," Hendry says.

The C-130 has four engines, a high wing, and a big cargo door in its tail. The door drops down to make a cargo ramp. The WC-130 is outfitted with special weather-measuring equipment. Otherwise, it is no different from the cargo version.

The C-130 has been improved several times over the years. Each new model is identified with a final letter. The original C-130 was built in the 1950s. It was dubbed the C-130A. The WC-130H has been the Hurricane Hunters' plane since the 1970s. In 1999, the squadron received its first new C-130 in many years, the WC-130J. It is an updated WC-130H, with newer engines, cockpit displays, and other improvements.

The C-130 Hercules has a large cargo door in its tail. Here, the ramp is down to allow an ambulance to roll out.

Specifications for
WC-130H[5]

Primary function—Weather reconnaissance

Manufacturer—Lockheed-Martin Corporation

Engines—Four turboprop engines

Wingspan—132 feet, 7 inches

Length—99 feet, 6 inches

Height—38 feet, 6 inches

Maximum takeoff weight—155,000 pounds

Range—4,000 miles

Maximum altitude—33,000 feet

Endurance—15 hours at 300 miles per hour

Maximum speed—Over 350 miles per hour

Crew—Two pilots, navigator, flight engineer, weather officer, and dropsonde system operator, who measures atmospheric conditions

CHAPTER 3

Hurricane Hunters at Work

The 53rd Weather Reconnaissance Squadron is part of the Air Force Reserve. Reservists are a part of the military, but in peacetime they usually wear their uniforms only during their two weeks of annual duty. The Hurricane Hunters schedule their duty time during the hurricane season, when they are most needed. They also volunteer extra time when they are needed, with the cooperation of their civilian employers.

Travis White is a civilian airline pilot. He is also an Air Force Reserve major. He earned his Air Force wings in 1988 and flew C-130 cargo planes in the active-duty Air Force. Since leaving active duty, he has continued to serve as a reservist with the Hurricane Hunters. "The majority of our missions happen in the summer, so it's sort of a summer job," he says.[1]

The squadron has ten WC-130s and twenty crews to fly them. Each crew has six positions: pilot, copilot, navigator, flight engineer, weather officer, and dropsonde system operator. The last two positions are special to the hurricane hunting missions.

Weather officer Dan Darbe calculates the wind speed on the surface of the ocean by observing the wave patterns.

The weather officer analyzes data collected by the airplane's onboard measuring equipment. Eight times per second, the equipment measures the airplane's position, the outside air (barometric) pressure, wind speeds, temperature, and humidity.

With trained eyes, the weather officer also adds his or her own observations. For example, the weather officer can look at the waves, foam, and spray on a storm-tossed ocean and estimate how strong winds are at the surface.

≡ Weather Station in a Can

The dropsonde system operator drops weather-measuring devices called dropsondes into the storm. The

Dropsonde operator Master Sergeant Burt Burril loads the dropsonde into the launch tube. As it falls to the surface of the ocean, the dropsonde measures temperature, barometric pressure, humidity, and wind speed and direction.

dropsonde is a one-pound cylinder, about the size of three large soup cans stacked end on end. It contains a tiny weather station, a battery, and a radio transmitter.[2]

The dropsonde system operator puts the dropsonde in a launching tube that looks like a pipe sticking up from the deck of the airplane. Inside the launching tube is a spring that shoves the dropsonde out of the bottom of the plane.[3]

Ten seconds after it drops out, the dropsonde releases a parachute that slows its descent. As it falls, it radios measurements back to the plane—barometric pressure, wind speeds, temperature, and humidity. It gives conditions inside the storm all the way down to the surface, where it falls into the sea. A WC-130 may drop several dropsondes on a single mission. A dropsonde costs about five hundred dollars, but it is only used once. There is no way to recover it from the ocean.[4]

The hurricane hunting equipment does not fill the Hercules. It still has a lot of room left in its big cargo hold. The room comes in handy when an approaching storm turns the Hurricane Hunters into the hunted. Their base at Biloxi is right on the Gulf of Mexico's northern coastline. Hurricanes can threaten that area, too, and force the squadron to load up its planes and flee.

"The last time we had to do that was for Hurricane Georges in 1998," Hendry says. "That hurricane hit our hometown after it ripped through the Caribbean [islands]. In 1995, our busiest season, we had to evacuate our home base four times."[5]

CHAPTER 4

NOAA's Storm Trackers

The 53rd Weather Reconnaissance squadron is not the only hurricane hunting unit in the United States. The National Oceanic and Atmospheric Administration (NOAA) has its own fleet of research airplanes. They include two WP-3D Orion aircraft. Like the WC-130s, they are rugged, four-engine airplanes.

The WP-3Ds are based at NOAA's Aircraft Operations Center at MacDill Air Force Base in Tampa, Florida, on the Gulf of Mexico. The unit used to be based on Florida's eastern coast at Miami International Airport. Hurricane Andrew wiped out its Miami facilities in 1992.[1]

The four-engine Orions are the biggest planes in NOAA's fleet. They fly missions all around the world, from the Arctic Ocean to the Tropics. Like the WC-130s, WP-3Ds track major storms. But their mission is broader. They gather a wide range of data to help scientists understand how weather works. This includes information about conditions in the atmosphere that can affect weather in future seasons.

For instance, the WP-3Ds have flown missions over the Pacific Ocean to study a weather phenomenon known as El Niño. El Niño is a vast body of warm water that forms from time to time in the Pacific Ocean. It has a huge

WP-3D Orions are four-engine planes that fly weather missions around the world.

It looks like a menacing claw, but the probe extending in front of this WP-3D Orion is used to gather data about the atmosphere.

effect on weather. It triggers floods and droughts in different parts of the United States.[2]

The WP-3D carries many instruments not found on the WC-130. For example, it carries three radars to probe the clouds. It also carries a larger crew of about eighteen people to operate the extra gear.[3]

≡ Low and Dangerous

Like the Air Force Reserve's Hurricane Hunters, NOAA's crews fly their WP-3Ds right through hurricanes. Both organizations fly low-altitude missions as the storms are developing. The WP-3Ds continue flying as low as 1,500

The instruments in the cockpit of a NOAA WP-3D aircraft allow pilots to fly as low as 1,500 feet above sea level.

feet above sea level when the storms reach hurricane strength. Their data help weather scientists develop computer programs that are used to predict the behavior of hurricanes.

So close to the sea's surface, WP-3D pilots work hard to keep their planes level as they plow through powerful updrafts and downdrafts. Says NOAA Commander Philip M. Kenul, a WP-3D pilot: "It's a constant game as you're flying through the storm. It's like a bad elevator ride and you can't get off it."[4]

Kenul has flown more than one hundred flights into more than twenty different hurricanes. He has had some rough rides. But he said a flight through Hurricane Hugo in 1989, before he joined the unit, has become a legend among the WP-3D crews.

≡ Unseen Threat

The airplane was making the first pass of the day through the storm. The crew entered Hugo 1,500 feet above the churning waves. "All the reports they got was that it was pretty mild," Kenul says. But embedded in the hurricane was an unseen threat: a tornado. The airplane hit it, and at the same moment one of its four engines quit.

The tornado rolled the airplane to the right and hurled it toward the ocean, Kenul said. The two pilots fought to control the plane. "At one point they stared at each other, wondering if this was the end," he said. They pulled the plane out of its dive just seven hundred feet—mere seconds—above the waves.

The plane reached the eye of the storm, where the air was calmer. But the pilots knew they would have trouble getting back out. They dumped fuel to lighten the plane and circled. They stayed inside the eye while they slowly climbed with one dead engine. They depended on reports from other airplanes inside the hurricane to guide them out.

"The back of the plane looked like it had been vandalized," Kenul says. Storage lockers had popped open. Soda cans and supplies were everywhere. A two-hundred-pound life raft, shackled to the floor, had broken loose. It had hit the cabin ceiling with such force that it had dented a metal handrail. "One guy got off the plane and never flew again," Kenul says.[5] An inspection found the airplane in good shape, Kenul says, but years later that handrail was still bent, a reminder of what nature can do.

The WP-3Ds, like the WC-130s, are ordinary airplanes that were built for other missions. The P-3 is a Navy plane built to patrol the oceans for enemy vessels. NOAA bought new P-3s from Lockheed in 1975 and 1976.[6] Kenul says nothing special was needed to toughen the WP-3Ds against hurricanes, "except they beefed up the deck a little bit" to hold the weather equipment.

Commander Philip M. Kenul is a WP-3D pilot. He has flown more than one hundred flights into hurricanes.

≡ Three Radars

Outside, the most striking feature about each of the WP-3Ds is a black pill-shaped object under its belly. It is one of the airplane's three radars. The others are in its nose and tail. The radars beam radio signals into the clouds. Their echoes indicate how much rain and moisture the clouds hold.

A NOAA WP-3D has a pill-shaped radar housing under the plane. There is a sensor-studded boom sticking out in front of the airplane that contains sensors for weather measurement, and a bulb-shaped radar housing in the tail.

Each airplane carries an assortment of equipment to study storms and other weather conditions. Like the WC-130s, the WP-3Ds carry dropsondes to measure conditions at all levels in a storm. The WP-3Ds also carry ocean current probes and devices called bathythermographs. Instead of measuring air, these instruments plop into the ocean and transmit data about ocean currents and temperatures. Water temperatures help forecasters predict how strong a storm will become, because warm ocean water is a source of energy for tropical storms. Scientists measure currents to understand how heat moves through the ocean.[7]

Some of the instruments used to gather data about the atmosphere are mounted under the wing of NOAA's WP-3D Orion.

Turboprops and Jets

Propeller airplanes might seem old-fashioned to people used to flying on jet airliners. The WC-130s and WP-3Ds have jet engines, but the engines have propellers. This type of engine is commonly called a turboprop. The engine produces a jet exhaust, but some of the exhaust goes through a turbine that turns a propeller.

Commander Philip Kenul says turboprop engines are good for hurricane hunting because they respond faster to power changes than pure jet engines. That is important in storms where the winds are constantly changing, because Hurricane Hunter pilots have to

Specifications for WP-3D[8]

Primary function—
Atmospheric research, weather reconnaissance

Manufacturer—
Lockheed-Martin Corporation

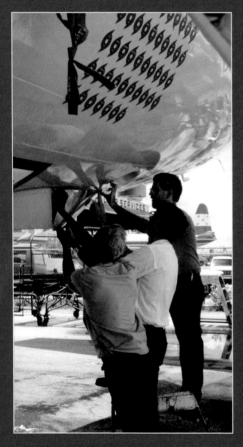

Technicians work on a NOAA WP-3D between flights. The red objects on the side of the aircraft indicate how many tropical storm missions the airplane has flown.

Engines—
Four turboprop engines

Wingspan—99 feet, 7 inches

Length—111 feet, 2 inches

Height—33 feet, 8 inches

Maximum takeoff weight—135,000 pounds

Range—4,100 miles

Maximum altitude—27,000 feet

Endurance—12 hours

Cruising speed—345 miles per hour

Crew—Two pilots, flight engineer, navigator, flight director (meteorologist), electronic engineer, electronic technician, radio operator, up to twelve scientists or observers

change engine power quickly to keep their speed steady while the weather researchers take measurements.[9]

But pure jets can fly higher and faster than airplanes with propellers. NOAA's newest hurricane hunter is a jet. Since 1997, NOAA's Gulfstream IV-SP has been flying around hurricanes at high altitudes. The sleek white-and-blue jet adds to the data that help forecasters sharpen their predictions.

The twin-engine Gulfstream IV, or G-IV, was designed as a business jet. It cruises at 45,000 feet above sea level.

Designed as a business jet, the Gulfstream IV helps during hurricane missions by circling the storm and gathering upper atmosphere data.

It can cover more than 4,600 miles on a single flight. Instead of flying through hurricanes, it flies around them to gather information about weather conditions in the upper atmosphere. This gives forecasters additional clues about how the hurricane is developing. It also helps scientists learn more about the natural processes that create hurricanes.

Like its sister WP-3Ds, the G-IV drops out dropsondes. Inside the airplane, the plush furnishings for business executives have been replaced by scientific equipment and eight workstations.

Specifications for
Gulfsteam IV-SP[10]

Primary function— Hurricane reconnaissance

Manufacturer— Gulfstream Aerospace Corporation

Engines—Two jet engines

Wingspan—77 feet, 10 inches

Length—88 feet, 4 inches

Height—24 feet, 5 inches

Maximum takeoff weight—74,600 pounds

Range—4,600 miles

Maximum altitude— 45,000 feet

Endurance— 9 hours + reserve

Cruising speed— 520 miles per hour

Crew—Two pilots, plus up to eight weather researchers

CHAPTER 5

At the Edge of Space

*H*igh above hurricanes flies the ER-2. Its long, slender wings make it look like a glider. It needs long wings to stay aloft in the top fringes of Earth's atmosphere. The ER-2 cruises at 65,000 to 70,000 feet, or twelve to thirteen miles above sea level. It flies higher than almost any other airplane in the world.

The ER-2 carries only one person, the pilot. The pilot is outfitted like a space shuttle astronaut. He wears a pressure suit and a space helmet. At the altitudes the ER-2 flies, the air outside is almost as thin as it is in outer space.

There are two ER-2s. They belong to NASA. NASA is better known for its space shuttles and space probes, but it also operates a fleet of airplanes for scientific missions. The ER-2s are important parts of its fleet.

The ER-2 carries cameras and other devices to observe Earth's lands and oceans. Its sensors collect data about the upper atmosphere. ER-2s have gathered information on natural processes ranging from the growth patterns of ocean life to major natural disasters, including earthquakes, volcanoes, and hurricanes.[1]

You could say the ER-2 is a spy plane for science. It is the same basic airplane as the famous Lockheed U-2 spy plane. Instead of spying on enemy countries, the ER-2 snoops on nature's secrets.

The sleek ER-2 is NASA's high-altitude plane. Its cameras observe our planet's lands and seas, while its sensors collect weather data.

≡ Designed for Spying

The U.S. Central Intelligence Agency had the U-2 developed in the 1950s to spy on the Soviet Union. The Soviet Union included Russia and several other countries. It was very secretive. U.S. leaders feared it was planning a surprise attack. The Lockheed Corporation designed the U-2 to fly above what they thought was the reach of enemy aircraft and missiles. Its high altitude also allowed the U-2 to photograph large areas on a single flight.

A Soviet missile knocked down a U-2 in 1960. That ended spy plane flights over the Soviet Union. U.S. spy satellites soon took up the job, but the U-2 was still useful for missions that did not take it directly over enemy land,

Pilot Jim Barrilleaux wears a pressure suit and a space helmet when he flies at high altitudes in the ER-2.

or where U.S. combat jets could protect the plane from attack.

In 1971, NASA began flying two old U-2Cs for scientific missions. Its first flights tested instruments to be used on new Earth-observing satellites. NASA used the U-2Cs until 1989.

Meanwhile, the original U-2 spy plane design was improved. The new model was called the U-2R. NASA bought two new U-2Rs in 1981 and 1989. They were larger and could carry a heavier payload. These are the ER-2s NASA flies today.[2]

"The difference between an ER-2 and a U-2 is the color of the paint and the payloads that we carry," says Jim Barrilleaux, an ER-2 pilot who flew Air Force U-2s before joining NASA.[3] Instead of the U-2's cloak-and-dagger black, NASA's ER-2s are painted lab-coat white with blue trim.

≡ Tricky to Fly

The ER-2 is a tricky airplane to fly, Barrilleaux says. The takeoff alone is like no other. The ER-2's wings are so long that two small wheels, called outriggers, help prop them up while the airplane is on the ground. They fall out of the wings when the airplane takes off.

ER-2 flights last from an hour and a half to nine hours. The pilot, already confined inside his bulky pressure suit, is strapped into the cockpit throughout the flight. "You feel like you're almost wearing the airplane," Barrilleaux says. "It's a long time in a small place. You can't stand up."[4]

Of course, there's no bathroom. "There is a way to pass fluids in the suit, but number two's a no-no," Barrilleaux says.

ER-2 pilots have to be careful not to eat or drink too much, but they cannot afford to get too dry or to run out

"The ER-2 is a tricky airplane to fly," says pilot Jim Barrilleaux. During the entire flight, the pilot is strapped into the cockpit.

of energy. How do you eat or drink with a helmet around your head? Barrilleaux says U-2 and ER-2 pilots carry water in a plastic squeeze bottle with a straw. The straw fits through a small, one-way opening in the helmet. They also eat food that is soft like baby food. It is packed in tubes so that pilots can suck it through a straw. On long flights, Barrilleaux says he slurps mushed-up apple pie, peaches, puddings, and meaty foods like sloppy joe.

Essential Safety Gear

The pressure suit and helmet are uncomfortable, but they are essential safety gear. The higher above sea level, the lower the air pressure and the less oxygen there is to breathe. At the ER-2's cruising altitudes, you would die almost instantly without protection. There is far too little oxygen to breathe, but that is not all. The air pressure is so low that your blood vessels would burst and your blood would bubble.[5]

The ER-2's cockpit gives some protection. It is pressurized to about a fifth of normal sea-level air pressure. That is thick enough to allow the ER-2 pilot to fly without inflating his pressure suit. There still is not enough oxygen in air that thin, so the pilot breathes pure oxygen inside his suit.

The thin air can still cause a serious problem. Rising to lower atmospheric pressures too quickly after breathing pressurized air can cause crippling pain. Deep-sea divers discovered this long ago and called it the bends. It happens because the air we breathe is mostly nitrogen, and some nitrogen is always dissolved in our blood. If the pressure around us drops too quickly, the nitrogen will start to bubble out and build up in our joints, causing severe pain.

An ER-2 pilot breathes pure oxygen before he flies to flush most of the nitrogen out of his body. Still, a pilot high in the sky sometimes feels the bends coming on. Unless he can descend immediately, his only choice is to inflate his pressure suit.

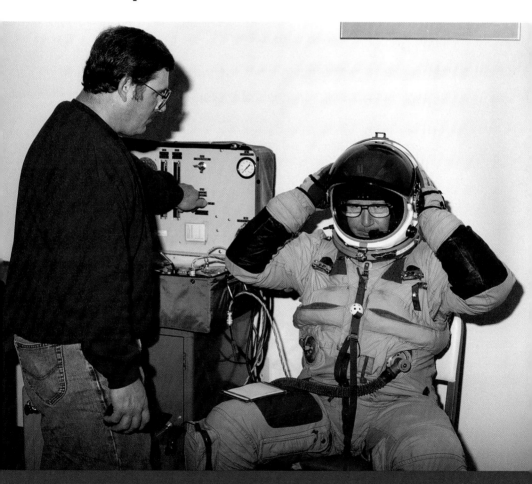

Pilot Jim Barrilleaux suits up at the Dryden Flight Research Center in California before his record-breaking ER-2 flight in 1998. He flew to 68,700 feet. Pilots breathe pure oxygen before the high-altitude flights to flush nitrogen from their bodies.

"All of us have flown with the suit inflated," Barrilleaux says. "When that happens, it's very difficult to move your hands and arms and legs. It's not something that any of us do for pleasure. But, when you have to do it, you do it."

Landing is the hardest thing about flying an ER-2. Its long wings make the airplane want to keep gliding. Barrilleaux says the pilot has to slow the airplane down until it quits flying, but he has to do it within three feet of the runway surface. Any higher, and the airplane will land too hard and be damaged.

It is all the trickier to keep the airplane going straight down the runway because the ER-2's main wheels are positioned with one pair in front of the other under its narrow body. "It's a tough airplane to land," Barrilleaux says.

Viewing Earth

But the view from an ER-2 cockpit a dozen miles above Earth is worth all the trouble. Earth's surface no longer looks flat, but curved. The daytime sky is darker. "You cannot see stars, but it is kind of a navy blue," Barrilleaux says.[6]

Even so, Barrilleaux says, a pilot can see many details on the ground. "You can still see mountains and rivers and towns. I can even see semi trucks driving down highways."

The view at night is different but equally dramatic. "At night, there seems to be hundreds of times the number of stars that you can see from the ground. I mean, everywhere you look, there's just stars everywhere," he says.

The tremendous view is a big reason why scientists use the ER-2. Its cameras and sensors can cover large areas of Earth yet still pick out fine details.[7]

Specifications for
ER-2[8]

Primary function—High-altitude scientific research
Manufacturer—Lockheed-Martin Corporation
Engine—one jet engine
Wingspan—103 feet, 4 inches
Length—62 feet, 1 inch
Height—16 feet
Payload—2,700 pounds
Range—3,400 miles
Maximum altitude—70,000 feet
Cruising speed—460 miles per hour
Crew—One pilot

The high-flying ER-2 also has helped scientists gather evidence of global changes caused by pollution. In the late 1980s and early 1990s, ER-2 flights over the North and South Poles helped show how human-made chemicals are breaking down the ozone layer in Earth's upper atmosphere.

The ozone layer is like Earth's sunblock: It prevents harmful levels of ultraviolet light from reaching the surface. As a result of the ER-2 flights and other research, the United States and other nations are cutting back the production and use of chemicals that can harm the ozone layer.

For ages, humans dreamed of flying through the sky like the birds. The Wright brothers learned the secrets of flight at the beginning of the twentieth century. Now that people know how to fly, they are using flight to understand the sky itself.

Weather research is demanding work. It is adventurous, and sometimes it is dangerous. Whether they are plunging through storms or soaring high over them, weather research aviators enjoy the challenge their work brings. NASA pilot Jim Barrilleaux has been flying U-2s and ER-2s for more than twenty-five years. He says he is still learning to be a better pilot. "I don't have the sense that I've done all there is that I could do with this airplane."[9]

The challenge is not the only reason these pilots and flight crew members do what they do. Travis White, a Hurricane Hunter pilot, sums it up simply: "What appeals to me is that we're out there helping people."[10]

Chapter Notes

Chapter 1. Into the Eye

1. National Oceanic and Atmospheric Administration, *Hurricanes*, "Hurricane Basics," n.d., <http://hurricanes.noaa.gov/prepare/> (May 7, 2000).

2. National Climate Data Center, "Hurricane Andrew," August 11, 1997, <http://www.ncdc.noaa.gov/ol/satellite/satelliteseye/hurricanes/andrew92/andrew.html> (December 1, 2000).

3. Ibid.

4. Author interview with U.S. Air Force Reserve Major Valerie J. Hendry, May 12, 2000.

5. National Oceanic and Atmospheric Administration.

6. 53rd Weather Reconnaissance Squadron, "Weather Reconnaissance," *Fact Sheet*, October 1999, <http://www.hurricanehunters.com/facrec.htm> (May 9, 2000).

Chapter 2. Tough Planes for a Tough Job

1. U.S. Air Force Reserve, *A History of the 53rd Weather Reconnaissance Squadron*, "53rd WRS History - The First Flight," n.d., <http://www.hurricanehunters.com/ohair.htm> (May 13, 2000).

2. Author interview with U.S. Air Force Reserve Major Valerie J. Hendry, May 12, 2000.

3. Author interview with U.S. Air Force Reserve Major Travis White, May 18, 2000.

4. U.S. Air Force Reserve, *A History of the 53rd Weather Reconnaissance Squadron*, n.d., <http://www.hurricanehunters.com/history2.htm> (May 13, 2000).

5. U.S. Air Force Reserve, "WC-130 Aircraft," *Fact Sheet*, October 1997, <http://www.hurricanehunters.com/fac130.htm> (May 14, 2000).

Chapter 3. Hurricane Hunters at Work

1. Author interview with U.S. Air Force Reserve Major Travis White, May 18, 2000.

2. Author interview with U.S. Air Force Reserve Major Valerie J. Hendry, May 12, 2000.

3. White.

4. Author interview with National Oceanic and Atmospheric Administration Commander Philip M. Kenul, July 1, 1999.

5. Hendry.

Chapter 4. NOAA's Storm Trackers

1. Author interview with National Oceanic and Atmospheric Administration Commander Philip M. Kenul, July 1, 1999.

2. Ibid.

3. National Oceanic and Atmospheric Administration, "NOAA's Hurricane Hunter Aircraft," *Fact Sheet*, February 1999, <http://www.publicaffairs.noaa.gov/grounders/hunter99.html> (May 7, 2000).

4. Kenul.

5. Ibid.

6. NOAA Aircraft Operations Center, "Lockheed WP-3D Orion," *Fact Sheet*, n.d., <http://www.nc.noaa.gov/aoc/aoc.html> (May 26, 2000).

7. NOAA Aircraft Operations Center, "Frequently Asked Questions," n.d., <http://www.nc.noaa.gov/aoc/data.html> (May 25, 2000).

8. NOAA Aircraft Operations Center, "Lockheed WP-3D Orion."

9. Kenul.

10. Gulfstream Aerospace Corp., "Gulfstream IV SP—Specifications," *Fact Sheet*, n.d., <http://www.gulfstream.com/prod/givsp/spec.htm> (May 27, 2000).

Chapter 5. At the Edge of Space

1. NASA, "NASA ER-2 High-Altitude Airborne Science Program" (Edwards, California: Dryden Flight Research Center, May 1998), pp. 1–2, 6.

2. Ibid., p. 1.

3. Author interview with ER-2 pilot Jim Barrilleaux, February 10, 2000.

4. Ibid.

5. Timothy R. Gaffney, "Pressure Chamber," *Boys' Life*, November 1993, p. 10.

6. Barrilleaux.

7. NASA, pp. 4, 7.

8. NASA Dryden Flight Research Center, "ER-2 Capabilities and Performance," *Fact Sheet*, n.d., <http://www.dfrc.nasa.gov/Projects/airsci/general/er-2/er2perf.html> (February 5, 2000).

9. Barrilleaux.

10. Author interview with U.S. Air Force Reserve Major Travis White, May 18, 2000.

bathythermograph—A device dropped into the ocean to measure its temperature.

bends—A condition marked by pain or paralysis caused by going from an atmosphere of high pressure to one of lower pressure, so that nitrogen in the body forms bubbles that collect in the joints.

dropsonde—A device that measures atmospheric conditions and radios the data to a receiving station as it falls through the air. Also called a dropwindsonde.

eye—A calm patch of sky at the center of a hurricane.

hurricane—An intense tropical weather system with a well-defined circulation and sustained winds of 74 miles per hour or higher. Hurricanes are called typhoons in the western Pacific and cyclones in the Indian Ocean.

meteorologist—A scientist who studies the atmosphere, including weather.

NOAA—National Oceanic and Atmospheric Administration. The U.S. agency responsible for forecasting weather and natural disasters.

pressure suit—An airtight suit that can be inflated to protect its wearer at high altitudes.

reconnaissance—A search for useful military information.

Soviet Union—A country that included what is now Russia and several other countries.

tropical depression—An organized weather system of clouds and thunderstorms with a defined circulation and sustained winds no higher than 38 miles per hour.

tropical storm—An organized system of strong thunderstorms with a defined circulation and sustained winds of 39 to 73 miles per hour.

turbine—A machine with a rotor that is driven by moving fluids (gases or liquids).

turboprop engine—An engine that uses exhaust gases to drive a turbine, which spins a propeller.

Further Reading

Ayres, Carter M. *Pilots and Aviation*. Minneapolis: Lerner, 1990.

Bilstein, Roger E. *Flight in America: From the Wrights to the Astronauts*. Baltimore: Johns Hopkins University Press, 1994.

Mackie, Dan. *Flight*. Burlington, Ontario: Hayes Publications, 1986.

Yount, Lisa. *Women Aviators*. New York: Facts on File, 1995.

Internet Addresses

53rd Weather Reconnaissance Squadron. *The Hurricane Hunters*. March 13, 2001. <http://www.hurricanehunters.com>.

National Oceanographic and Atmospheric Administration. *NOAA.gov*. April 10, 2001. <http://www.noaa.gov>.

National Oceanographic and Atmospheric Administration. *Aircraft Operations Center*. March 21, 2001. <http://www.hurricanehunters.noaa.gov/aoc.html>.

National Oceanographic and Atmospheric Administration. *National Hurricane Center*. April 10, 2001. <http://www.nhc.noaa.gov>.

National Aeronautics and Space Administration. *Dryden Flight Research Center*. April 10, 2001. <http://www.dfrc.nasa.gov>.